Self-Employed HELOC Strategies

How Business Owners, 1099 Borrowers, and LLCs Unlock Home Equity

By Joseph G. Correa

Licensed Mortgage Broker, Finibi Mortgage

Copyright & Legal Notice

First Edition, 2026

Table of Contents

Foreword

For the self-employed, money flows differently. Income is not handed to you on a bi-weekly paycheck. It arrives in waves, in invoices, in deposits, in merchant statements, in retainers, in commissions, and sometimes in silence between deals. Yet the modern mortgage system was built for salaried employees, not entrepreneurs. It rewards predictability over profitability, simplicity over reality, and W-2s over business ownership. This mismatch is why so many highly successful business owners are told they "don't qualify" when they try to access their own home equity. This book exists to correct that injustice. It is written for the millions of Americans who do not fit inside a bank's narrow box but who, in truth, are among the most financially powerful people in the economy. If you are a contractor, consultant, realtor, doctor, investor, Uber driver, digital entrepreneur, content creator, or small business owner operating through an LLC or S-corp, your financial profile is not broken. It is simply misunderstood. And misunderstood borrowers are often the most profitable borrowers—when they know how to navigate the system.

Over the years, I have watched self-employed borrowers walk into banks with strong businesses, significant assets, and six-figure incomes, only to walk out defeated because a tax return showed deductions or a business had a complex structure. The truth is that smart entrepreneurs legally reduce their taxable income. They depreciate assets, expense equipment, and invest back into growth. That makes them better business owners, but it often makes them appear "weaker" on paper. This book will show you how lenders actually look at income for self-employed borrowers, how to present your financials correctly, and how to use specialized programs that were created specifically for business owners. There is a massive difference between being denied by a retail bank and being approved by a lender who understands how entrepreneurs really earn money. Once you understand that difference, the entire world of home equity opens up to you.

A Home Equity Line of Credit, or HELOC, is one of the most powerful financial tools available to business owners. It allows you to tap into the value you have already built in your home without selling it, refinancing it, or triggering a taxable event. For entrepreneurs, this means instant access to flexible capital that can be used to stabilize cash flow, invest in growth, buy inventory, fund marketing, hire staff, acquire rental properties, or seize opportunities when they appear. Traditional business loans are slow, rigid, and often require extensive documentation. A properly structured HELOC can give you access to capital in days, not months, with interest rates that are often far lower than credit cards, merchant cash advances, or unsecured lines of credit. When used correctly, it becomes a private banking system for your business—one that you control.

This book is not about gaming the system or cutting corners. It is about understanding the system so you can use it intelligently. You will learn how bank statement loans work, how lenders calculate income from deposits instead of tax returns, how LLCs and S-corps can qualify for HELOCs, and how to structure your finances to present the strongest possible profile. You will also learn how to avoid the traps that cause so many self-employed borrowers to get declined, such as mis-timed tax filings, poorly structured business accounts, or mixing personal and business funds. These details matter. In the mortgage world, the difference between approval and denial is often not how much money you make, but how clearly that money can be documented and understood by the lender reviewing your file.

As a licensed mortgage broker working with business owners and investors every day, I have seen how transformative home equity can be when it is unlocked the right way. I have watched entrepreneurs use HELOCs to rescue struggling businesses, fund six-figure marketing campaigns, buy investment properties, launch online brands, and create generational wealth. I have also seen what happens when borrowers are given bad advice or take on the wrong type of debt. This book will teach you not just how to get a HELOC, but how to use it strategically, safely, and in alignment with your long-term goals. Home equity should be a tool that supports your business, not a risk that threatens your home.

If you are self-employed, your income is often more powerful than a paycheck because it is scalable. You are not limited by hours worked or a fixed salary. Your business can grow, your clients can multiply, and your revenue can expand without a ceiling. When you combine that type of income with the leverage of home equity, you gain something truly rare: the ability to convert stability into opportunity. Your home becomes more than a place to live. It becomes a financial engine. It becomes the foundation beneath your entrepreneurial vision. That is what this book is really about—teaching you how to turn what you already own into the fuel that drives what you want to build.

By the time you finish this book, you will understand how lenders evaluate self-employed borrowers, how to position yourself for approval, and how to design a HELOC strategy that fits your business model. Whether you are a solo freelancer or the owner of multiple LLCs, the principles in these pages will give you clarity, confidence, and control. The financial world was not designed for entrepreneurs, but it can absolutely work for them when they know the rules. This book will show you those rules, and how to use them to unlock the true power of your home equity.

Chapter 1

How Self-Employed Income Is Really Calculated for HELOCs

For self-employed borrowers, the first and most dangerous mistake is believing that lenders look at income the same way they do for W-2 employees. They do not. A salaried worker hands over pay stubs and a W-2 and the job is done. A business owner, however, is evaluated through an entirely different lens. Lenders are not asking, “How much did you make?” They are asking, “How much stable, predictable, and usable income does this business generate after expenses?” That distinction is what causes so many self-employed borrowers to get denied even when they are profitable. The lender is not trying to punish you for deductions. They are simply trying to determine how much of your income is available to support debt. Understanding this mindset is the foundation of everything that follows.

Tax returns are the starting point for most traditional lenders. They look at Schedule C, K-1s, 1120S forms, and business tax filings to see what the business produced after expenses. If you grossed $250,000 but deducted $190,000 in expenses, the lender does not see a $250,000 business. They see a $60,000 business. That $60,000 becomes your qualifying income, regardless of how much cash actually flowed through your bank accounts. This is why many self-employed borrowers feel like the system is unfair. They are told they only make $5,000 a month when their business deposits $20,000 a month. The difference is depreciation, write-offs, and business strategies that lower taxes but also lower qualifying income. The lender is not wrong. They are simply following a formula that was never designed for entrepreneurs.

This is why bank statement HELOCs exist. Instead of relying on tax returns, these programs look at your actual cash flow. The lender reviews 12 or 24 months of business or personal bank statements and calculates your average monthly deposits. Those deposits become the starting point for income. Some lenders then apply an expense factor, such as 50 percent or 30 percent, to estimate how much of those deposits represent usable income. This is far more realistic for business owners. If you deposit $30,000 per month and the lender applies a 50 percent expense ratio, they count $15,000 per month as your income. That is far more accurate than a tax return showing $6,000 after write-offs. This method allows strong businesses to qualify for much larger HELOCs without changing how they file taxes.

LLC and S-corp owners have another advantage. These entities allow income to be paid in multiple ways, such as owner distributions, payroll, and retained earnings. Some HELOC lenders allow business income to be counted even if it is not all paid out to you personally. If your LLC earns $300,000 and you only pay yourself $120,000, a bank statement HELOC may still recognize the higher cash flow depending on how the funds move through the business account. This is why separating business and personal finances is critical. When all income flows cleanly through a business account, it becomes far easier to prove financial strength to a lender.

Consistency matters just as much as volume. Lenders want to see stable deposits, not huge spikes followed by dry months. A contractor who deposits $18,000 every month for a year will qualify far more easily than one who deposits $80,000 one month and $2,000 the next. HELOCs are revolving lines of credit, and lenders want to know that you can reliably make the minimum payments even when business slows down. This is why timing your HELOC application during a strong income period is so important. Your last twelve months of deposits may determine whether you get a $75,000 line or a $400,000 line.

Credit still plays a role, but it is not the dominant factor for self-employed borrowers. In bank statement HELOC programs, income and equity are more important than perfect credit. A borrower with a 680 score and strong cash flow can often qualify when a borrower with a 760 score but weak deposits cannot. Equity also matters. Most HELOCs allow borrowing up to 85 or 90 percent of your home's value when combined with your existing mortgage. The more equity you have, the more room lenders have to work with.

What this all means is that self-employed borrowers must think strategically. The goal is not just to make money, but to make that money visible and predictable to lenders. Deposits, account structure, consistency, and documentation determine whether your home equity is locked or unlocked. Once you understand how income is calculated, you can design your business finances to support your borrowing goals. This is not manipulation. It is alignment. You are simply making sure your financial reality is properly reflected on paper.

By mastering these rules, you gain the ability to access six figures or even seven figures in revolving credit without selling your home or refinancing your mortgage. That is the power that lies ahead in this book. Everything starts with income, and now you know how lenders really see it.

Practical Example: *How a Self-Employed Borrower Qualifies for a $250,000 HELOC*

Imagine a business owner named Carlos who runs a digital marketing agency through an LLC. Carlos works with small businesses and charges monthly retainers. His business deposits fluctuate, but over the last year he has averaged $28,000 per month in deposits into his business bank account. That means his total annual deposits are $336,000. On his tax return, however, Carlos shows only $110,000 in net income after deducting advertising, software, contractors, home office, vehicle, and depreciation. A traditional bank would use $110,000 to qualify him. That equals about $9,166 per month. After subtracting his mortgage, car payment, and credit cards, he would not qualify for much more debt. He might get denied completely.

Instead, Carlos applies for a bank statement HELOC. The lender reviews 12 months of his business bank statements and confirms that the average monthly deposit is $28,000. The lender applies a 50 percent expense factor, which is common for service businesses. This means they assume $14,000 per month is usable income. That equals $168,000 per year for qualifying purposes. This is already $58,000 higher than what his tax return showed. Now the lender looks at Carlos's debts. His mortgage payment is $2,600 per month. His car payment is $600. His credit cards total $400 in minimum payments. That means his total monthly obligations are $3,600.

Next the lender calculates debt-to-income ratio. With $14,000 in qualifying income and $3,600 in monthly debt, Carlos's DTI is 25.7 percent. Most HELOC lenders allow DTIs up to 45 or even 50 percent. This means Carlos has room for much more debt. If the lender allows a 45 percent DTI, Carlos can have total monthly obligations of $6,300. He already has $3,600, so he can support an additional $2,700 per month in HELOC payment.

Now we look at the home. Carlos owns a house worth $700,000. He owes $350,000 on his first mortgage. That means he has $350,000 in equity. Most HELOC programs allow borrowing up to 85 percent of the home's value. Eighty-five percent of $700,000 is $595,000. Subtract his $350,000 mortgage and he has $245,000 in available equity. That means the maximum HELOC he can get based on equity is $245,000.

Next we check affordability. A $245,000 HELOC at 9 percent interest, interest-only, would have a payment of about $1,837 per month. That is well below his available $2,700 in capacity. That means Carlos qualifies for the full equity-based HELOC amount. The lender approves a $245,000 revolving HELOC.

Carlos now has access to nearly a quarter million dollars without selling his house, without refinancing his mortgage, and without proving tax return income. If he draws $100,000, he only pays interest on that $100,000. If he pays it down, his credit line becomes available again. He uses the HELOC to fund a $50,000 marketing campaign, $30,000 in new hires, and $20,000 in equipment. Those investments increase his monthly deposits to $40,000 within six months. Because the HELOC is revolving, he can later refinance or expand it based on the higher income.

This is how business owners turn their homes into growth engines. The numbers are not magic. They are math, cash flow, and equity working together. Once you understand how lenders calculate income, you can design your finances to unlock the full power of your home.

Chapter 2

Structuring Your Business and Bank Accounts to Qualify for Larger HELOCs

Self-employed borrowers do not get approved or denied because of how much money they make. They get approved or denied based on how clean, predictable, and verifiable their money looks to a lender. The same business earning the same revenue can qualify for wildly different HELOC amounts depending on how the accounts are structured. This is why many entrepreneurs unknowingly sabotage their borrowing power. They mix personal and business funds, accept payments in multiple apps, move money between accounts randomly, or fail to maintain consistent deposit patterns. From a lender's perspective, this creates noise. And noise creates risk. When a lender sees confusion, they reduce income, add overlays, or decline the loan entirely.

The first rule of HELOC optimization for business owners is separation. Your business must have its own bank account, and all business income should flow into that account before being transferred to your personal account. Lenders using bank statement programs look at deposits. They do not guess. They calculate. If $300,000 runs through your business account but only $120,000 ever moves to your personal account, many lenders will only count the $120,000 if you apply using personal statements. If you apply using business statements, they may count the full $300,000 minus an expense factor. This difference alone can double or triple your qualifying income. The account you choose matters as much as the money itself.

Consistency is the next lever. Lenders want to see recurring deposits that reflect ongoing operations. If your deposits jump from $5,000 to $80,000 and back down to $3,000, your income will be averaged and often reduced. A business that deposits $18,000 every month for a year is far more attractive than one that deposits $200,000 in one month and almost nothing in the others. This is because HELOCs are revolving lines. The lender is not concerned about how much you made last year. They care whether you can make payments this year, next year, and the year after. Stability equals confidence.

The third lever is how your business pays you. LLCs and S-corps allow distributions, draws, payroll, and retained earnings. Some HELOC programs require that a portion of the income flow into your personal account to be counted. Others do not. If you are planning to apply for a HELOC, it is often beneficial to increase the consistency of owner draws for several months before applying. This creates a visible income trail that aligns your business success with your personal finances. You are not changing reality. You are aligning reality with how lenders measure it.

Another powerful factor is deposit sourcing. Lenders categorize deposits. Revenue deposits from clients are counted as income. Transfers from other accounts, loans, and cash infusions are not. If you constantly move money from savings, PayPal, Venmo, or other accounts into your main account, the lender may remove those deposits from the calculation. The cleanest statements are those where most deposits clearly come from customer payments. This is why funneling all revenue through a single operating account before paying expenses or transferring profits creates a stronger income profile.

The final element is seasoning. HELOC lenders usually want 12 to 24 months of bank statements. What you do today affects what you can borrow next year. This means strategic planning matters. Entrepreneurs who understand this will adjust how they move money, pay themselves, and collect revenue months before applying. Those who do not often wait until the last minute and then wonder why the numbers do not work. A HELOC is not a last-minute loan. It is the reward for disciplined financial presentation.

When all of these elements come together, a business owner

can qualify for far more than their tax return would ever allow. Their real income is no longer hidden behind write-offs or accounting strategies. It becomes visible, stable, and lendable. That is how home equity is unlocked at scale.

Practical Example: *How Account Structure Turned a $90,000 HELOC Into a $310,000 HELOC*

Consider a self-employed real estate photographer named Megan who operates as a single-member LLC. Megan shoots photos, videos, and virtual tours for realtors. Her clients pay through Stripe, Zelle, and checks. Over the last year, Megan's business generated $360,000 in revenue. However, her financial setup was messy. Some clients paid into her business account. Others paid into her personal account. She transferred money back and forth to pay bills. On paper, her personal account showed $140,000 in deposits and her business account showed $220,000. When she first applied for a HELOC using her personal bank statements, the lender saw $140,000 in annual deposits, which equals $11,666 per month. After applying a 50 percent expense factor, the lender counted $5,833 per month as income.

Megan owned a $650,000 home with a $400,000 mortgage. That gave her $250,000 in equity. At 85 percent loan-to-value, she could borrow up to $552,500 total, meaning she had $152,500 in potential HELOC. But income limited her. With

$5,833 per month in qualifying income and $3,200 in existing debts, she only had $2,633 left. That supported about a $90,000 HELOC. She was shocked.

Instead of accepting that result, Megan cleaned up her accounts. For the next 12 months, she required all clients to pay into her business account. Every month she transferred a consistent $12,000 to her personal account as owner draw. Her business account now showed $30,000 in monthly deposits. Her personal account showed $12,000 in monthly income. When she reapplied, she used her business statements. The lender averaged $30,000 per month and applied a 40 percent expense factor because photography has lower overhead. That meant $18,000 per month in qualifying income.

Her debts were still $3,200. With $18,000 in income, she could support up to $8,100 in total obligations at a 45 percent DTI. That meant she had $4,900 available for a HELOC payment. Her equity still allowed $152,500, but now income allowed much more. At 9 percent interest, $152,500 required about $1,144 per month. She easily qualified.

But the story did not end there. Megan's home had appreciated to $750,000. At 85 percent, that allowed $637,500 total. Subtract her $400,000 mortgage and she now had $237,500 in HELOC capacity. That payment was about $1,780 per month, still far below her $4,900 limit. She was approved for the full $237,500.

Simply by restructuring how money flowed through her accounts, Megan increased her HELOC from $90,000 to over $237,000. The business did not change. The revenue did not change. Only the visibility of that revenue changed. That is how smart business owners turn accounting into leverage and turn home equity into a financial engine.

Chapter 3

How Lenders Use Debt-to-Income and Cash-Flow Analysis for Self-Employed HELOCs

For self-employed borrowers, the true gatekeeper to HELOC approval is not credit score, tax returns, or even equity. It is debt-to-income ratio, commonly called DTI, and its business cousin, cash-flow analysis. DTI is the percentage of your monthly income that goes toward paying debt. Lenders use this number to determine whether you can safely take on a new line of credit without default risk. Business owners often underestimate how powerful this calculation is because they focus on gross income instead of usable income. The difference between those two numbers is where most HELOC approvals are won or lost.

When a lender evaluates a W-2 employee, income is fixed. When they evaluate a business owner, income must be interpreted. This is why bank statement programs and alternative documentation exist. Once income is determined, the lender then lists every recurring debt: mortgage payments, car loans, student loans, credit cards, business loans that report to personal credit, and even child support or alimony if applicable. These obligations are totaled and divided by monthly income. The resulting percentage determines how much room remains for a HELOC payment. If the ratio is too high, the loan is denied regardless of equity.

Most HELOC lenders allow DTIs between 40 and 50 percent for strong borrowers. That means if your income is $15,000 per month, the total of all debts including the HELOC cannot exceed $6,000 to $7,500. If your current obligations are already $5,500, the HELOC payment can only be $500 to $2,000 depending on the program. This is why two borrowers with identical incomes can qualify for wildly different HELOCs. The one with fewer monthly debts can borrow far more.

For business owners, cash-flow analysis adds another layer. Some HELOC lenders do not just look at deposits. They look at how much money remains after business expenses. If your business deposits $25,000 per month but spends $23,000, the lender may not count all of that income. This is why profitability matters just as much as revenue. Strong cash flow shows that the business is not just busy, but healthy.

One of the biggest hidden killers of HELOC approvals is business debt that shows up on personal credit. Many entrepreneurs use personal credit cards, personal loans, or even HELOCs to fund their businesses. Lenders count these payments against personal DTI even if the business makes the money. This can severely reduce borrowing power. A business owner earning $20,000 per month but paying $4,000 in business credit cards on their personal report may be treated like a heavily indebted consumer instead of a thriving entrepreneur.

This is why restructuring debt is often more powerful than earning more income. Paying off or refinancing high monthly payments can instantly unlock hundreds of thousands of dollars in HELOC capacity. Lowering a car payment from $1,200 to $500 increases borrowing power by the same amount as raising income by $1,400. Cash-flow engineering is just as powerful as revenue growth.

Lenders also stress-test HELOC payments. Because HELOCs have variable rates, lenders often calculate the payment using a higher interest rate than today's rate. This protects them against rising rates and protects you from over-borrowing. The stronger your income and cash flow, the more flexibility you have.

Understanding DTI and cash-flow math allows self-employed borrowers to take control. You no longer guess what you qualify for. You can calculate it. When you know the numbers, you can decide when to apply, how much to borrow, and what financial moves will maximize your home equity power.

Practical Example: *How Cash-Flow and DTI Turned a Denial Into a $420,000 HELOC*

David owns a construction company and operates through an S-corp. His business deposits an average of $45,000 per month. Using bank statements, the lender applies a 40 percent expense factor, meaning 60 percent is counted as income. That gives David $27,000 per month in qualifying income. That equals $324,000 per year.

David owns a $900,000 home with a $450,000 mortgage. At 85 percent loan-to-value, he can borrow up to $765,000 total. Subtracting his $450,000 first mortgage gives him $315,000 in available HELOC equity. That means equity alone limits him to $315,000. However, income must also support the payment.

David's debts include his mortgage at $3,200 per month, two trucks financed on his personal credit at $1,400 each, and credit cards with $1,000 in minimum payments. That totals $7,000 per month. At a 45 percent DTI limit, David can have total obligations of $12,150. That leaves $5,150 available for a HELOC payment.

At 9 percent interest, a $315,000 HELOC would require about

$2,362 per month. David easily qualifies. However, the lender also includes a stress-test rate of 11 percent, which would make the payment $2,887. That is still well below his $5,150 limit. David is approved for the full $315,000.

Six months later, David refinances his trucks into business-only loans that no longer report on his personal credit. His personal debt drops by $2,800 per month. His new monthly obligations are $4,200. With the same $27,000 income, his 45 percent limit remains $12,150, meaning he now has $7,950 available for HELOC payments.

His home value rises to $1,000,000. At 85 percent, he can now borrow $850,000. Subtracting his $450,000 mortgage gives $400,000 in HELOC capacity. At 9 percent, $400,000 costs $3,000 per month. He qualifies easily. By managing cash flow and debt structure, David turned a $315,000 HELOC into a $400,000 revolving line of capital without increasing his income by a single dollar.

Chapter 4

How Equity, Appraisals, and Loan-to-Value Determine Your HELOC Power

For self-employed borrowers, income gets you in the door, but equity determines how much money you are allowed to take out. Equity is the portion of your home that you truly own, calculated as the market value minus any loans secured against it. Lenders use this number to protect themselves and you. A HELOC is not based on how much you need. It is based on how much your home can safely support. Understanding how this calculation works gives you direct control over how much capital you can unlock.

Every HELOC is governed by loan-to-value, known as LTV. LTV is the percentage of your home's value that is borrowed. If your home is worth $600,000 and you owe $300,000, your LTV is 50 percent. Most HELOC lenders allow a combined loan-to-value, called CLTV, between 80 and 90 percent. That means the total of your first mortgage and HELOC cannot exceed that percentage of the home's value. If a lender allows 85 percent CLTV on a $600,000 home, the total allowed debt is $510,000. Subtract the existing mortgage, and the difference is the maximum HELOC. Appraisals or valuation models determine the home's value. Some lenders use full appraisals, others use automated valuation models, and some use hybrid methods. Self-employed borrowers benefit greatly from accurate valuations because even small increases in value create large increases in HELOC capacity. A $50,000 increase in home value at 85 percent CLTV creates $42,500 in new borrowing power. This is why timing your HELOC after a period of appreciation or after making improvements can dramatically increase your line size.

Equity is not just about market value. It is also about how fast you are paying down your mortgage. Every payment increases your ownership. Self-employed borrowers who aggressively reduce their first mortgage are quietly building a future borrowing engine. That equity can later be converted into business capital without refinancing or selling the property. A HELOC allows you to keep your low-rate mortgage intact while using the equity as flexible funding.

Many entrepreneurs make the mistake of pulling out cash through refinances instead of HELOCs. Refinancing replaces your entire mortgage with a new one, often at a higher rate, and resets the amortization. A HELOC sits on top of your existing mortgage and only charges interest on what you use. This preserves long-term wealth while providing short-term liquidity. The smarter your equity management, the more powerful this tool becomes.

Some self-employed borrowers also own multiple properties. Lenders may allow HELOCs on primary residences, second homes, and sometimes investment properties. Each property is evaluated separately, and the total equity across your portfolio can become a massive pool of capital. Entrepreneurs who understand this use their real estate as a private banking system. They move capital from property to business and back again as needed, always keeping their equity working.

The key is that equity is not static. It grows with appreciation, principal payments, and smart renovations. When you understand how lenders calculate it, you can plan ahead, increase value, reduce balances, and time your HELOC strategically. Your home is not just shelter. It is a balance sheet.

Practical Example: *How Home Value and LTV Created a $520,000 HELOC*

Rachel owns a consulting firm and is self-employed. She bought her home five years ago for $550,000 with a $440,000 mortgage. Over time, she has paid the loan down to $390,000. The neighborhood has also appreciated, and homes now sell for about $820,000. Her equity is calculated by subtracting her loan from her home value. That is $820,000 minus $390,000, which equals $430,000. Rachel applies for a HELOC with a lender that allows 85 percent CLTV. Eighty-five percent of $820,000 is $697,000. That means the total of her first mortgage and HELOC cannot exceed $697,000. Since she owes $390,000, the maximum HELOC she can have is $307,000. That is $697,000 minus $390,000.

Six months later, Rachel renovates her kitchen and bathrooms, spending $60,000 from savings. The home is now appraised at $900,000. Eighty-five percent of $900,000 is $765,000. Her mortgage is still $390,000, so her new HELOC limit is $375,000. The renovation created $68,000 of new borrowing power, because $900,000 times 0.85 is $765,000 and $765,000 minus $390,000 equals $375,000.

Rachel also makes an extra $2,000 payment toward her mortgage every month for a year, reducing the balance by $24,000. Her mortgage drops to $366,000. Her home value remains $900,000. The 85 percent limit is still $765,000. Now her HELOC capacity becomes $399,000, calculated as $765,000 minus $366,000. By improving her home and paying down debt, she increased her HELOC from $307,000 to $399,000 without changing her income at all.

Rachel then buys a second home for $600,000 with a

$420,000 mortgage. It appraises at $650,000 a year later. At 80 percent CLTV, she can borrow $520,000 total. Subtracting the $420,000 mortgage gives $100,000 in HELOC capacity on that property. Combined with her primary residence, Rachel now has nearly $500,000 in available revolving capital.

This is how self-employed borrowers turn real estate into financial infrastructure. The math is simple, but the impact is enormous.

Chapter 5

How to Choose the Right HELOC Program for Self-Employed Borrowers

One of the biggest mistakes self-employed borrowers make is assuming that all HELOCs are the same. They are not. In fact, the program you choose often matters more than your income or your credit score. Different lenders use different documentation methods, expense factors, loan-to-value limits, rate structures, and underwriting rules. Choosing the wrong program can cost you hundreds of thousands of dollars in available credit even if you qualify on paper. Choosing the right program can unlock far more equity with less stress and less paperwork.

The most common HELOC is the traditional full-documentation HELOC. This version uses tax returns, W-2s, pay stubs, and standard debt-to-income ratios. For a self-employed borrower who aggressively writes off expenses, this is usually the worst choice. A business earning $300,000 may only show $90,000 in taxable income, which dramatically limits borrowing power. Traditional HELOCs also tend to have tighter debt-to-income limits and lower combined loan-to-value caps. They work best for salaried borrowers, not entrepreneurs.

The second major category is the bank statement HELOC. This is the preferred tool for most self-employed borrowers. These programs look at 12 or 24 months of business or personal bank statements and calculate income based on deposits rather than tax returns. The lender then applies an expense ratio, often between 30 and 50 percent depending on the industry. This method recognizes how real businesses operate and almost always produces higher qualifying income than tax returns. It also allows for more flexibility in income patterns, which is critical for business owners.

The third category is the asset-based or no-doc HELOC. These programs focus almost entirely on equity and credit. Income is either not verified or lightly reviewed. These HELOCs often allow very high loan-to-value ratios, sometimes up to 90 percent, but they usually carry higher interest rates. They are ideal for borrowers with strong equity and imperfect income documentation, such as investors, high-net-worth individuals, or entrepreneurs in volatile industries. For some self-employed borrowers, this is the fastest and easiest path to capital.

Rate structure is another critical factor. Some HELOCs are interest-only, which keeps payments low and preserves cash flow. Others require principal and interest, which reduces the line over time but increases monthly payments. A business owner focused on cash flow usually prefers interest-only. Draw periods and repayment periods also matter. A longer draw period means you can use and repay the line repeatedly, making it function more like a credit card secured by your home.

Fees, closing costs, and prepayment penalties also vary widely. Some HELOCs cost nothing to open. Others charge thousands. Some lock you in for years. Others allow you to close or refinance at any time. These terms directly impact your ability to move, sell, or refinance your home later.

The smartest self-employed borrowers treat HELOCs as financial instruments, not just loans. They compare programs the way investors compare stocks. The goal is not just approval. The goal is maximum flexibility, lowest cost, and highest usable capital. Once you understand the menu of options, you stop being a borrower and start being a strategist.

Practical Example: *Choosing the Right HELOC Turned $180,000 Into $460,000*

Mark owns a landscaping company and operates as an LLC. His business deposits average $32,000 per month, or $384,000 per year. After expenses, his tax return shows only $120,000 in net income. Mark owns a home worth $850,000 and owes $420,000 on his mortgage. His available equity at

85 percent CLTV is $722,500 minus $420,000, which equals $302,500. Mark first applies for a traditional HELOC using tax returns. The lender uses $120,000 per year, or $10,000 per month, as income. His debts total $5,500 per month. At a 43 percent DTI, he can only have $4,300 in total obligations. Since he already has $5,500, he is denied. A different lender allows 50 percent DTI, giving him $5,000 allowed debt, but he still exceeds it. He is told he can only qualify for about $180,000 if he pays off some debt.

Mark instead applies for a bank statement HELOC. The lender averages $32,000 per month in deposits and applies a 40 percent expense ratio, giving him $19,200 in qualifying income. With $5,500 in debt, he is at 28.6 percent DTI. At a 45 percent limit, he can have $8,640 in total obligations, leaving $3,140 for a HELOC payment. At 9 percent interest, that supports about $420,000 in HELOC, but equity caps him at $302,500. He qualifies for the full $302,500.

Mark then compares an asset-based HELOC that allows 90 percent CLTV. Ninety percent of $850,000 is $765,000. Subtracting his $420,000 mortgage leaves $345,000 in available equity. This program requires minimal income documentation. The payment on $345,000 at 10 percent is $2,875, which is still below his $3,140 cash-flow capacity. Mark qualifies for $345,000. Finally, Mark waits six months as his home value rises to $980,000. At 90 percent CLTV, that allows $882,000 in total debt. Subtracting his $420,000 mortgage gives $462,000 in HELOC capacity. By choosing the right program and timing his application, Mark turns what would have been a $180,000 HELOC into a $462,000 revolving line of capital without changing his business at all.

Chapter 6

How to Use a HELOC to Stabilize, Scale, and Protect Your Business

For self-employed borrowers, a HELOC should never be treated as just another loan. It is a financial control system. When used correctly, it becomes a shock absorber for cash-flow swings, a growth engine for expansion, and a safety net that prevents emergencies from turning into disasters. Most businesses fail not because they are unprofitable, but because they run out of liquidity at the wrong moment. A HELOC solves that problem by giving you immediate access to capital without forcing you to sell assets, take on predatory loans, or dilute ownership.

Cash-flow volatility is the defining feature of entrepreneurship. One month you may collect $60,000, the next only $15,000. Fixed expenses do not disappear just because revenue dips. Rent, payroll, software, insurance, and debt still have to be paid. A HELOC allows you to smooth those cycles. Instead of panicking or using high-interest credit cards, you draw from your HELOC during slow months and pay it down during strong months. This turns irregular income into something that feels almost salaried. You are no longer at the mercy of timing. The second power of a HELOC is speed.

Business opportunities rarely wait. Equipment deals expire. Inventory discounts vanish. Properties go under contract. Marketing windows close. Traditional loans are slow and uncertain. A HELOC is instant. Once it is open, the money is yours to deploy at any moment. This allows self-employed borrowers to act like large institutions instead of small operators. Speed creates profit, and profit repays the line.

A HELOC also lowers your cost of capital. Credit cards often charge 20 to 30 percent. Merchant cash advances can exceed 50 percent annually. Even business lines of credit often run in the teens. HELOC rates are typically far lower. This means the same business investment becomes dramatically more profitable simply because the interest expense is lower. The goal is not to borrow more. The goal is to borrow smarter.

Risk management is just as important. A HELOC should never be maxed out without a plan. The smartest entrepreneurs keep unused credit available as a buffer. That unused capacity is insurance. It protects against slow seasons, client losses, equipment failures, and market shifts. A business with liquidity can survive almost anything. A business without liquidity collapses even when profitable.

A HELOC also allows you to restructure bad debt. High-interest business credit cards, short-term loans, and expensive equipment financing can often be paid off using the HELOC. This lowers monthly payments, improves cash flow, and strengthens DTI for future borrowing. One good HELOC can clean up an entire financial balance sheet.

When you combine stability, speed, and low cost, your home equity becomes something far more powerful than a loan. It becomes the financial backbone of your business. Used wisely, it allows self-employed borrowers to grow faster, survive longer, and operate with far less stress.

Practical Example: *How a HELOC Turned Cash-Flow Chaos Into a Stable $250,000 Business Engine*

Anthony owns a mobile auto-detailing company. His revenue swings wildly based on weather and seasonality. In the summer he earns $40,000 per month. In the winter he drops to $15,000. His fixed business expenses are $18,000 per month, including payroll, van leases, insurance, and software. In winter, he loses money even though the business is profitable over the year.

Anthony owns a home worth $700,000 with a $380,000 mortgage. At 85 percent CLTV, he can borrow $595,000 total. Subtracting his mortgage gives him $215,000 in HELOC capacity. He opens a $200,000 HELOC.

During slow winter months, Anthony draws $3,000 per month from the HELOC to cover payroll and overhead. Over four months, he draws $12,000. At 9 percent interest, the monthly interest on $12,000 is only $90. In summer, he earns $40,000 per month and repays $4,000 per month for three months, fully paying off the balance.

Anthony then uses $60,000 from the HELOC to buy two new vans and equipment instead of leasing. The leases would have cost $2,200 per month. The HELOC interest on $60,000 at 9 percent is $450 per month. He saves $1,750 every month. That savings allows him to hire another crew, which increases revenue by $18,000 per month.

Within a year, the business generates an additional $216,000 in revenue. Even after paying interest of about $5,400 on the $60,000 balance, the return is massive. Anthony keeps $155,000 in unused HELOC capacity as emergency reserves.

What started as home equity becomes a permanent financial safety net and growth fund. This is how self-employed borrowers turn real estate into a private banking system.

Chapter 7

How to Recycle HELOC Capital to Multiply Business Growth Without Taking on New Debt

The most powerful feature of a HELOC is not that it lets you borrow money. It is that it lets you reuse money. This is called capital recycling, and it is what turns a HELOC from a loan into a growth engine. When most people borrow, they think in one direction. They take money, spend it, and then slowly pay it back. Business owners who understand capital recycling think in loops. They deploy money into income-producing assets, use the cash flow from those assets to repay the HELOC, and then reuse the same line again to fund the next opportunity. The debt does not grow. The assets do.

Traditional loans trap capital. A business loan gives you $100,000, you spend it, and you are stuck with a fixed balance for years. A HELOC is different. If you borrow $100,000, use it to generate profit, and pay it back, the $100,000 becomes available again. That means one HELOC can fund ten projects instead of one. Over time, the same line of credit can move millions of dollars through your business without ever being permanently consumed. The key to safe capital recycling is cash-flow alignment. You should only deploy HELOC funds into things that produce predictable income within a reasonable time frame. That could be inventory that sells within 60 days, a marketing campaign that brings clients within weeks, equipment that increases monthly revenue, or rental properties that generate rent. The faster the money comes back, the safer the strategy becomes. Long-term speculative investments are not ideal uses for HELOC funds.

This method also dramatically reduces risk. Because the HELOC is revolving, you never need to accumulate permanent debt. You are temporarily using the bank's money to create profit and then returning it. This is how large corporations operate. They use revolving credit lines to fund operations and growth while keeping long-term debt low. Self-employed borrowers can do the same thing with their home equity.

Interest becomes a business expense instead of a burden. If you borrow $80,000 at 9 percent and it generates $12,000 per month in revenue, the interest is irrelevant. The goal is not zero interest. The goal is positive spread, where the money you earn exceeds the cost of capital. That spread becomes profit.

The smartest entrepreneurs also maintain unused HELOC capacity as a safety buffer. Even if you have $300,000 available, you may only use $150,000 at any time. The remaining $150,000 is your protection against unexpected opportunities or emergencies. This is how HELOCs provide both growth and security.

Capital recycling allows you to grow faster without ever becoming trapped by debt. You are not borrowing to survive. You are borrowing to multiply. When done correctly, your HELOC balance will go up and down, but your business income will only go up.

Practical Example: *How One $150,000 HELOC Created Over $1 Million in Business Growth*

Sophia owns a digital education company that sells online courses. She opens a $150,000 HELOC on her home at 9 percent interest. The monthly interest on $150,000 is about $1,125 if fully drawn. She never draws the full amount at once. Instead, she uses it strategically.

Sophia first draws $50,000 to run paid advertising. Over three months, the ads generate $180,000 in course sales. Her profit margin after expenses is 40 percent, so she nets $72,000. She repays the $50,000 HELOC balance and keeps $22,000 in profit. Her HELOC is back to zero.

Next, she draws $60,000 to hire a sales team and upgrade her platform. Over four months, revenue increases by $300,000. At a 35 percent margin, she earns $105,000. She repays the $60,000 and keeps $45,000.

She then uses $80,000 from the HELOC to launch a new product. That launch generates $500,000 in sales over six months with a 30 percent margin, producing $150,000 in profit. She repays the $80,000 and keeps $70,000.

Over one year, Sophia used the same HELOC three times, moving $190,000 through it. The total revenue generated was $980,000. The total profit was $247,000. The total interest paid across all draws was about $7,000. That means a $150,000 HELOC created nearly a quarter million dollars in net income without permanent debt.

This is capital recycling. The HELOC is never the destination. It is the engine.

Chapter 8

How to Use a HELOC to Create Long-Term Passive Income as a Self-Employed Borrower

For self-employed borrowers, the ultimate goal of a HELOC is not just to fund operations or short-term growth. The true power of home equity is revealed when it is converted into assets that generate income without daily labor. This is how business owners transition from working for money to having money work for them. A HELOC gives you access to low-cost, flexible capital that can be deployed into investments that produce monthly cash flow. When structured correctly, those cash flows can pay the HELOC down while leaving you with permanent income streams.

Passive income is not about doing nothing. It is about doing something once that continues to pay you over time. Rental properties, dividend-paying investments, revenue-generating websites, equipment leasing, and private lending are all examples of income streams that can be funded with HELOC capital. The key is that these assets must produce predictable monthly income that exceeds the HELOC interest and principal payments. When that condition is met, the HELOC becomes self-liquidating. The investment pays for the debt that created it.

The biggest mistake self-employed borrowers make is chasing appreciation instead of cash flow. Appreciation is uncertain and cannot be used to make HELOC payments. Cash flow is what makes the system safe. If you invest $100,000 from your HELOC into something that produces $1,500 per month and your HELOC interest on that balance is $750, the investment pays for itself and leaves $750 in surplus. That surplus can be used to pay down the principal faster, creating equity while also creating income.

Real estate is one of the most common uses of HELOC-funded investing. A HELOC can be used for down payments, renovations, or full purchases of small rental properties. Because the HELOC is interest-only in most cases, the carrying cost is low, allowing rental income to cover both the HELOC and the property's own expenses. Over time, the tenant pays off the investment while the owner keeps the equity.

Private lending is another powerful strategy. Business owners often lend HELOC funds to other investors at 10 to 15 percent while paying 7 to 9 percent on the HELOC. The difference is pure profit. The principal remains intact, meaning the same HELOC funds can be redeployed repeatedly. The long-term goal is not to keep a HELOC balance forever. It is to use the

HELOC to create assets that eventually replace it. When the investments are paid off, the HELOC can be closed or left open as a safety net. At that point, the homeowner owns both the house and the income streams.

This is how self-employed borrowers transform home equity into financial independence. The house stops being a static asset and becomes the foundation of a permanent income machine.

Practical Example: *How a $200,000 HELOC Created $8,500 per Month in Passive Income*

Jonathan owns an e-commerce consulting firm. He opens a $200,000 HELOC on his home at 8.5 percent interest. If he draws the full amount, the interest-only payment is about $1,417 per month. Jonathan uses the HELOC to fund three income-producing investments.

First, he uses $80,000 as a down payment on a duplex that costs $400,000. The mortgage payment, taxes, and insurance on the duplex total $2,200 per month. The two units rent for $2,000 each, producing $4,000 per month. After expenses, the property generates $1,800 per month in cash flow. That $1,800 covers the HELOC interest on the $80,000 portion, which is about $567 per month, leaving $1,233 in net profit. Next, Jonathan lends $70,000 from his HELOC to a real estate flipper at 12 percent interest. That produces $700 per month. The HELOC interest on $70,000 is about $496. The spread is $204 per month.

Then he uses $50,000 to buy a content website that produces $3,500 per month in advertising and affiliate income. After $500 in expenses, it nets $3,000. The HELOC interest on $50,000 is about $354, leaving $2,646 per month.

Now we add the numbers. The duplex generates $1,800. The private loan generates $700. The website generates $3,000. That equals $5,500 per month in gross passive income. The HELOC interest on the full $200,000 is $1,417. Subtracting that leaves $4,083 in net positive cash flow.

Jonathan applies $2,000 of that surplus to pay down the HELOC principal every month. At that rate, he pays off the $200,000 in about 8.3 years. When the HELOC is gone, he still owns the duplex, the website, and the note, which together continue to generate $5,500 per month. That is $66,000 per year in permanent passive income created from home equity.

This is how self-employed borrowers use HELOCs to escape the cycle of working for money and build income that lasts.

Chapter 9

How to Protect Your Home, Credit, and Business When Using HELOC Leverage

Using a HELOC as a self-employed borrower creates extraordinary opportunity, but it also creates responsibility. Home equity is powerful because it is secured by your property. That means misuse does not just affect your business or your credit, it affects your home. The goal of a professional HELOC strategy is not just to grow faster, but to grow safer. Risk management is what separates disciplined wealth builders from people who lose everything in a downturn.

The first layer of protection is cash-flow discipline. A HELOC should only be used for things that either generate income or reduce expenses in a meaningful way. Borrowing against your home to buy depreciating consumer items or to cover chronic overspending is the fastest way to create financial stress. The line must be attached to productive uses. If the money does not come back, it does not belong in a HELOC strategy.

The second layer is reserve management. Smart borrowers never use their entire HELOC. They keep at least 30 to 50 percent of their line unused at all times. That unused credit is emergency liquidity. It protects against business slowdowns, client losses, medical emergencies, and market shocks. When the economy tightens, credit dries up. The HELOC you already have becomes priceless. Those who are fully drawn lose flexibility at exactly the wrong time.

The third layer is payment control. HELOCs usually have variable rates. When rates rise, payments rise. This means every HELOC strategy must work even at higher interest levels. If your investment or business only works at low rates, it is not safe. Your cash flow should be strong enough to handle rate increases without stress. Conservative projections protect your home.

The fourth layer is credit health. Late payments on a HELOC can destroy your credit profile and freeze access to future financing. Because HELOCs are revolving credit lines, high balances also affect utilization ratios. This can temporarily lower credit scores. Smart borrowers plan for this and do not apply for other major loans while their HELOC is heavily used.

The final layer is exit planning. Every HELOC strategy should include a clear path to repayment. Whether it is business cash flow, property sales, refinancing, or asset liquidation, you should know how the balance will eventually go to zero. Leverage is only dangerous when it has no exit.

When these rules are followed, HELOCs become safe, powerful

tools. When they are ignored, they become financial landmines. The difference is discipline.

Practical Example: *How Smart Risk Management Kept a $350,000 HELOC Safe During a Business Downturn*

Lena owns a marketing agency and has a $350,000 HELOC on her home at 8.75 percent interest. Her monthly interest-only payment when fully drawn would be about $2,552. Instead of using all of it, Lena limits herself to $200,000. That means her monthly interest is only $1,458, and she keeps $150,000 in unused credit as a safety buffer.

Lena invests $120,000 of the HELOC into advertising campaigns for her clients, which generate $30,000 per month in gross revenue. After paying contractors and expenses, her profit is $12,000 per month. She uses $4,000 to pay down the HELOC and keeps $8,000 as business income. The remaining $80,000 of her drawn HELOC is used to pay off high-interest business credit cards that were costing her $3,200 per month. The HELOC interest on that $80,000 is only about $583. This frees up $2,617 per month in cash flow.

Now a recession hits and client revenue drops by 40 percent. Her $12,000 profit falls to $7,200. But her HELOC payment obligation is still manageable because she only owes $200,000. Even if rates rise to 11 percent, the payment on

$200,000 would be about $1,833. She still has $5,367 left after interest.

Because Lena kept $150,000 unused, she is not forced to panic. She uses $20,000 of that buffer to keep operations running until revenue stabilizes. Once business improves, she pays it back.

By using only part of her HELOC, maintaining reserves, and focusing on cash-flow-positive investments, Lena protects her home while still growing her business. This is how leverage becomes a shield instead of a weapon.

Chapter 10

The Complete Self-Employed HELOC Blueprint for Long-Term Wealth and Control

At this point in the book, you understand how self-employed income is calculated, how accounts must be structured, how debt and cash flow affect approval, how equity limits borrowing, how to choose the right program, how to stabilize and grow your business, how to recycle capital, how to build passive income, and how to protect your home while doing it. This chapter brings all of those pieces together into one integrated blueprint. A HELOC is not a product. It is a system. When each part of that system is designed intentionally, it becomes one of the most powerful financial tools available to business owners.

The first step of the blueprint is visibility. Your income must be visible and consistent in bank statements. This means running all revenue through clean business accounts, paying yourself regularly, and minimizing unnecessary account transfers. The second step is leverage positioning. You reduce high monthly debt, clean up personal credit usage, and avoid unnecessary payments that weaken DTI. The third step is equity optimization. You track home value, make strategic improvements, and reduce mortgage balances so that your borrowing capacity grows every year. These three elements create the foundation for HELOC access.

Once the line is open, you do not rush to use it. You deploy capital only into projects that either produce income or eliminate expensive debt. You recycle the line instead of stacking new loans. You maintain reserves inside the HELOC and outside it. You stress-test your payments for higher interest rates. You always know your exit. This is how you stay in control even as your capital grows.

A self-employed borrower who follows this blueprint never becomes dependent on banks. The HELOC becomes a permanent source of liquidity. When markets tighten and credit disappears, your line is already open. When opportunities appear, your capital is ready. Over time, the assets you build with the HELOC replace the HELOC itself. You end up with income-producing assets and a paid-off home.

This is the true power of home equity for entrepreneurs. It is not about borrowing. It is about turning what you already own into the engine that builds what you want to own next.

Practical Example: *A Complete HELOC Wealth System in Action*

Michael owns a software consulting company and earns an average of $30,000 per month in business deposits. Using a bank statement HELOC, 50 percent of that is counted as income, giving him $15,000 per month. His home is worth $1,000,000 and he owes $480,000. At 85 percent CLTV, he can borrow $850,000 total, meaning he has $370,000 in HELOC capacity.

Michael opens a $350,000 HELOC but uses only $220,000. The interest at 9 percent on $220,000 is $1,650 per month. He uses $120,000 to buy a small apartment building that produces $2,800 per month in net cash flow. He uses $60,000 to fund marketing that increases business profit by $6,000 per month. He uses $40,000 to pay off business credit cards that were costing him $1,800 per month.

Now we add the cash flows. The apartment produces $2,800. The business growth adds $6,000. The debt payoff saves $1,800. That totals $10,600 per month. Subtract the HELOC interest of $1,650 and Michael has $8,950 in surplus cash flow.

He uses $5,000 per month to pay down the HELOC. In 44 months, the $220,000 balance is gone. When the HELOC is paid off, Michael still owns the apartment building, which produces $2,800 per month, and his business continues to generate $6,000 more per month than before. His home is untouched, his line is available again, and his income has permanently increased. This is the self-employed HELOC blueprint in action.

Chapter 11

How to Use HELOC Leverage to Build Multi-Entity Wealth and Financial Resilience

For self-employed borrowers who operate more than one business or investment entity, a HELOC becomes far more than a source of funding. It becomes the central liquidity hub for an entire financial ecosystem. Entrepreneurs often run multiple LLCs, partnerships, and investment vehicles, each with its own income, expenses, and credit profile. Most of those entities struggle with one thing: access to low-cost capital. Banks treat new or small entities as risky. A personal HELOC backed by home equity bypasses that problem entirely. It allows the owner to move capital into any entity at any time, regardless of that entity's age or credit history.

This creates what can be called private banking. Instead of begging lenders for approvals, the entrepreneur uses their home as a balance sheet and their HELOC as a treasury. Capital flows from the HELOC into businesses, investments, and projects that produce cash flow, and then flows back into the HELOC as profits are generated. Each entity becomes a contributor to the system. Over time, this creates diversification. If one business slows down, the others continue to produce income. The HELOC smooths out volatility across the entire portfolio.

One of the most powerful advantages of this structure is risk isolation. Each business operates in its own legal and financial silo, but the HELOC sits above them all as a flexible funding source. A failed venture does not destroy the whole system as long as the HELOC is not overused. This allows entrepreneurs to take calculated risks, knowing that no single bet can sink the ship.

Cash-flow stacking is another benefit. When multiple entities generate income, those streams can be combined to pay down the HELOC faster. Instead of relying on one business to service the debt, the entire ecosystem contributes. This accelerates deleveraging and increases safety.

Tax efficiency also improves. Interest paid on HELOC funds used for business or investment purposes is often deductible, depending on how the funds are used and documented. This lowers the effective cost of capital, increasing profitability across the portfolio.

The long-term goal is not permanent borrowing. It is permanent control. The HELOC allows the entrepreneur to deploy capital instantly, move money between entities, and build wealth without being dependent on outside lenders. Over time, the assets created with HELOC capital replace the need for the HELOC itself.

Practical Example: *How One HELOC Powered Three Businesses and Created $500,000 in Net Worth*

Olivia owns three businesses: a digital marketing agency, a small e-commerce brand, and a rental property LLC. Her home is worth $900,000 and she owes $400,000. At 85 percent CLTV, she can borrow $765,000 total, leaving $365,000 in HELOC capacity. She opens a $350,000 HELOC but limits her use to $220,000.

She allocates $80,000 to her marketing agency to hire staff and scale ads. That increases profit by $6,000 per month. She allocates $70,000 to her e-commerce brand to buy inventory, which increases profit by $4,000 per month. She uses $70,000 as a down payment on a rental property that produces $1,500 per month in net cash flow. Now we add the numbers. The agency produces $6,000. The e-commerce brand produces $4,000. The rental produces $1,500. That totals $11,500 per month.

The interest on $220,000 at 9 percent is $1,650 per month. Subtracting that leaves $9,850 in surplus. Olivia uses $6,000 per month to pay down the HELOC. In about 37 months, the $220,000 is paid off.

After that, Olivia still owns all three businesses and the rental property, which together continue to generate $11,500 per month. Her home remains intact. The HELOC is available again. Her net worth has increased by more than $500,000 through equity and business value.

This is how self-employed borrowers turn home equity into a multi-entity wealth engine.

Chapter 12

Turning Your HELOC Into a Permanent Personal Banking System

At the highest level, a HELOC is not a loan. It is a private banking system that allows a self-employed borrower to control the flow of money, reduce dependence on external lenders, and build wealth on their own terms. Traditional banks are designed to profit from keeping borrowers trapped in long-term debt. A HELOC, when used correctly, reverses that relationship. It allows you to use short-term leverage to create long-term assets, all while keeping full ownership and control.

The first principle of a personal banking system is liquidity. Liquidity means having access to capital at all times. When markets crash, banks stop lending. Credit cards are cut. Business loans are frozen. A HELOC that is already open cannot be taken away easily. It becomes your financial lifeboat. This is why experienced entrepreneurs prioritize opening HELOCs during good times, not bad times.

The second principle is velocity. Money that moves faster produces more. When income flows through your HELOC and then back into it, every dollar works multiple times. Instead of sitting idle in checking accounts, cash offsets interest and reduces balances. This lowers interest costs while increasing available credit. The faster money circulates, the more powerful the system becomes.

The third principle is control. You decide when to borrow, when to repay, and where to deploy capital. You are not waiting for loan approvals or underwriting. You already have access. This allows you to act quickly on opportunities and protect yourself from emergencies.

The final principle is compounding. Assets built with HELOC funds produce income. That income pays down the HELOC. When the HELOC is repaid, the assets remain. Over time, this creates a snowball effect where more assets produce more income, which creates more ability to borrow, invest, and repay. This is how entrepreneurs build financial independence.

When these principles are followed, your home becomes more than shelter. It becomes the core of a private financial system that grows stronger every year.

Practical Example: *Building a $1 Million Personal Banking System with One HELOC*

Ethan owns a consulting business and earns $25,000 per month. His home is worth $1,100,000 and he owes $500,000.

At 85 percent CLTV, he can borrow $935,000 total, leaving $435,000 in HELOC capacity. He opens a $400,000 HELOC and uses only $250,000.

He uses $100,000 to buy a rental property that produces $2,500 per month in net income. He uses $80,000 to fund business growth that increases profit by $6,000 per month. He uses $70,000 to lend privately at 12 percent, generating $700 per month.

Now we add the cash flows. The rental produces $2,500. The business produces $6,000. The private loan produces $700. That totals $9,200 per month. The interest on $250,000 at 9 percent is $1,875. Subtracting that leaves $7,325.

Ethan applies $5,000 per month to pay down the HELOC. In 50 months, the $250,000 is gone. When the HELOC is repaid, Ethan still owns the rental, the business cash flow, and the private note, which together produce $9,200 per month. That is over $110,000 per year in income created from home equity.

At that point, Ethan still has a $400,000 HELOC available. His home has appreciated. His income has increased. He now has a fully functioning personal banking system that can be used for the rest of his life.

Chapter 13

Using HELOCs to Create a Family Wealth and Legacy System

When a self-employed borrower understands HELOCs at a deep level, the focus naturally shifts from personal success to generational security. Home equity is not just a tool for business growth. It is a bridge between today's income and tomorrow's family wealth. When structured correctly, a HELOC allows families to build income-producing assets that survive beyond any single career, business, or market cycle. This is how wealth becomes permanent instead of fragile.

The greatest threat to family wealth is interruption. Jobs end, businesses fail, markets crash, and unexpected health or economic events can erase years of progress. A HELOC acts as a stabilizer because it provides liquidity that cannot be easily taken away. Even if income temporarily drops, access to capital allows families to continue paying bills, keeping assets, and staying invested instead of being forced to sell at the worst time.

The second role of a HELOC in a family system is education. When parents use home equity to create assets rather than consume, children grow up seeing money as a tool instead of a reward. Rental income, dividend flows, and business profits become part of the household. This changes how the next generation understands finance, risk, and opportunity.

The third role is succession. Businesses and investments created with HELOC capital can be passed down. The HELOC itself can be refinanced, repaid, or transferred as part of estate planning. When structured correctly, the assets outlive the debt. That is the foundation of legacy wealth.

The goal is not to borrow forever. The goal is to use borrowing to create things that make borrowing unnecessary in the future. When the HELOC is paid off, the family owns income-producing assets free and clear. At that point, the house is no longer just a place to live. It is the cornerstone of a multi-generation financial system.

This is how entrepreneurs turn effort into permanence.

Practical Example: *How One Family Turned Home Equity Into $2 Million of Long-Term Wealth*

Daniel and Maria own a home worth $1,200,000 with a $500,000 mortgage. At 85 percent CLTV, they can borrow $1,020,000 total, leaving $520,000 in HELOC capacity. They open a $500,000 HELOC but use only $300,000.

They use $150,000 to buy three rental properties that produce $4,500 per month in net income. They use $100,000 to invest in their family business, which increases profits by $7,000 per month. They use $50,000 to buy dividend-producing investments that generate $400 per month.

Now we add the numbers. The rentals produce $4,500. The business produces $7,000. The investments produce $400. That totals $11,900 per month. The interest on $300,000 at 9 percent is $2,250. Subtracting that leaves $9,650.

They apply $7,000 per month to pay down the HELOC. In about 43 months, the $300,000 is gone. When the HELOC is repaid, the family still owns three rentals, a stronger business, and a dividend portfolio. Those assets together continue producing $11,900 per month, or over $140,000 per year.

Over 20 years, even without growth, that income would exceed $2.8 million. The HELOC is gone. The home remains. The assets stay in the family. That is how HELOCs become legacy machines.

Chapter 14

Mastering the HELOC Cycle to Achieve Lifetime Financial Independence

At the highest level of financial mastery, a HELOC is not a loan, an investment tool, or even a banking system. It is a cycle. That cycle converts stability into opportunity, opportunity into income, income into equity, and equity back into opportunity again. This is how self-employed borrowers escape the limitations of linear income and build financial independence that does not depend on working more hours. The house becomes the anchor, and the HELOC becomes the engine.

The first phase of the HELOC cycle is accumulation. This is when you build equity through mortgage payments, appreciation, and strategic home improvements. You are quietly storing financial energy inside your property. Most homeowners see this as passive. Entrepreneurs see it as preparation. Every dollar of equity is future leverage that can be deployed.

The second phase is extraction. This is when you open or expand a HELOC. You are not taking money out of your home. You are converting equity into liquid capital. This allows you to move from a static asset into a dynamic one. Money that was locked in walls and land becomes available for business, investing, and opportunity.

The third phase is deployment. HELOC funds are placed into income-producing assets or business expansion. The goal is always cash flow first. Appreciation is secondary. Cash flow is what makes the system safe and repeatable. The money must come back.

The fourth phase is acceleration. Cash flow from investments and business is used to pay down the HELOC. This increases available credit while reducing risk. The faster this happens, the stronger the system becomes.

The final phase is compounding. Once the HELOC is paid down, the assets remain. Those assets produce more income, which can be used to build more equity, open larger HELOCs, and fund even bigger projects. Over time, this cycle creates exponential growth.

When repeated over decades, this process produces a level of financial independence that cannot be achieved with salaries or savings alone.

Practical Example: *How One HELOC Cycle Created $3 Million in Wealth*

Tyler owns a home worth $950,000 with a $400,000 mortgage. His equity is $550,000. At 85 percent CLTV, he can borrow up to $807,500. Subtracting his mortgage leaves $407,500 in HELOC capacity. He opens a $400,000 HELOC but uses only $250,000.

He uses $150,000 to buy rental properties that produce $4,500 per month in net cash flow. He uses $100,000 to expand his online business, increasing profit by $8,000 per month. The HELOC interest on $250,000 at 9 percent is $1,875 per month.

Now we calculate. The rentals produce $4,500. The business produces $8,000. That totals $12,500. Subtract the HELOC interest of $1,875 and Tyler has $10,625 remaining.

He applies $7,500 per month to the HELOC. In 34 months, the $250,000 is paid off. His home is untouched. His rental properties and business continue producing $12,500 per month.

After five years, Tyler's rentals appreciate to $700,000 and his business is worth $1.2 million. His home appreciates to $1.1 million. His net worth is now over $3 million — built by cycling equity, not by earning more hours. This is the HELOC cycle at work.

Chapter 15

Exiting the HELOC Cycle: Turning Leverage Into Permanent Wealth and Financial Freedom

The highest level of HELOC mastery is knowing when and how to stop using it. Borrowing is not the goal. Freedom is. The HELOC is a bridge between where you are and where you want to be. Once enough assets have been built, the bridge should no longer be needed. This chapter explains how self-employed borrowers convert temporary leverage into permanent wealth and exit the HELOC cycle without sacrificing liquidity or growth.

The first step of the exit strategy is asset stabilization. By this point, the HELOC has funded multiple income-producing assets, such as businesses, rental properties, private loans, and digital cash-flow streams. These assets should now be mature, profitable, and predictable. The focus shifts from expansion to optimization. Instead of reinvesting every dollar into new growth, the entrepreneur begins directing surplus cash flow toward eliminating the HELOC balance. The assets continue producing income, but that income is now used to buy back the house's equity. The second step is balance reduction. HELOC interest is variable. Eliminating that payment removes risk and increases monthly cash flow. As the balance declines, more of the monthly income becomes free and clear. This accelerates the payoff. It creates a positive feedback loop where less debt leads to more available cash, which leads to even faster debt elimination.

The third step is capital replacement. While the HELOC is being paid down, the entrepreneur builds liquid reserves outside the line. This could be cash, brokerage accounts, or business savings. Once the HELOC reaches zero, these reserves replace it as the new liquidity source. The difference is that these reserves are owned outright, not borrowed.

The final step is strategic refinancing or closure. Some borrowers keep the HELOC open with a zero balance as an emergency tool. Others close it entirely and rely on their assets. Either choice represents victory. The home is now free of HELOC debt, the assets remain, and the income continues.

This is how leverage becomes legacy.

Practical Example: *How a $500,000 HELOC Was Converted Into $4 Million in Permanent Wealth*

Carla owns a consulting firm and several rental properties. Ten years ago, her home was worth $1,200,000 and she owed $500,000. At 85 percent CLTV, she had $520,000 in HELOC capacity. She opened a $500,000 HELOC and used $350,000 over time.

She invested $200,000 into rental properties that produced $7,000 per month in net cash flow. She invested $100,000 into her business, increasing profits by $9,000 per month. She invested $50,000 into private lending at 12 percent, producing $500 per month. Her total new income was $16,500 per month.

The interest on $350,000 at 8.5 percent was $2,479. That left $14,021 per month. Carla applied $10,000 per month to the HELOC and lived on the rest. In 35 months, the $350,000 balance was gone.

At that point, Carla owned multiple rentals worth $1.8 million, a business valued at $1.5 million, and private notes worth $50,000. Her home was now worth $1.6 million and still had the original $500,000 mortgage. Her net worth exceeded $4 million.

She closed the HELOC. The assets remained. The income remained. The leverage disappeared. This is the endgame of smart HELOC strategy.

Final Thoughts

The purpose of this book was never to teach you how to borrow money. It was to teach you how to control money. Self-employed people live in a different financial universe than salaried workers. Your income is flexible, scalable, unpredictable, and powerful, but most banks are designed for people who earn the same amount every two weeks. That mismatch is why so many entrepreneurs are told no when they ask for capital, even when they are financially strong. This book exists to correct that imbalance by showing you how to translate your real financial strength into lender-recognized power.

Home equity is one of the few financial assets that grows quietly in the background of your life. While you are building businesses, serving clients, raising families, and paying down mortgages, your home is accumulating value through appreciation and principal reduction. Most people do nothing with that value until they sell or refinance, and by then they often use it for consumption instead of creation. Self-employed borrowers who understand HELOCs do the opposite. They treat home equity as working capital, not retirement savings. They convert it into businesses, investments, income streams, and long-term wealth. Throughout this book, you learned that income is not just what you make, but what you can prove. You learned how bank statements, account structure, consistency, and cash-flow discipline determine how lenders see you. You learned how equity and loan-to-value ratios shape how much you can access. You learned how debt-to-income, interest rates, and reserve management determine how safe leverage really is. Most importantly, you learned how to turn a HELOC into a system instead of a one-time loan.

The difference between dangerous debt and powerful leverage is intent. When borrowed money is used for consumption, it creates stress. When it is used to build income, it creates freedom. The HELOC strategies in this book are not about spending. They are about creating assets that pay for themselves and then keep paying long after the HELOC is gone. That is how temporary borrowing becomes permanent wealth.

What makes self-employed borrowers uniquely positioned for this strategy is that you control both sides of the equation. You control how income is generated and how it is deployed. You are not limited to fixed wages or employer benefits. You can scale your revenue, diversify your income streams, and move capital across businesses and investments. When that flexibility is combined with home equity, it creates a level of financial leverage that most people never experience. The real danger is not using a HELOC. The real danger is leaving equity idle while inflation erodes it and opportunities pass by. When used with discipline, a HELOC becomes a shock absorber for bad times, a turbocharger for good times, and a bridge to long-term financial independence. It allows you to stay liquid when others are forced to sell, to invest when others are afraid, and to build when others are stuck.

This book has given you the blueprint. What happens next depends on execution. Open your line during strong financial periods. Keep your accounts clean and your cash flow visible. Maintain reserves. Deploy capital into income-producing uses. Recycle profits. Pay down balances. Build assets. Repeat. Over time, the HELOC will disappear, but the wealth it created will remain.

That is the true goal. Not borrowing forever, but using borrowing to build something that lasts forever.

How to Get a Personalized HELOC Review

If you found *HELOC Fundamentals: How Home Equity Lines of Credit Really Work — and How to Use Them Safely* helpful, you may want to see how these concepts apply to your own home, credit profile, and financial goals. nnnnnn

Every homeowner's situation is unique. Home value, mortgage balance, credit history, income type, and state-specific lending rules all affect how much equity you can access, what type of HELOC you may qualify for, and what terms may be available. The examples in this book are designed to teach how HELOCs work — but your real options can only be determined by reviewing your actual numbers.

If you would like a **no-obligation Home Equity Line of Credit review**, you can request one here:

Website:https://www.nodocsheloc.com

Email: info@FinibiMortgage.com

A licensed mortgage broker will review your information and explain what HELOC and home equity options may be available to you based on your specific situation.

No cost. No pressure. No obligation.

Joseph G. Correa

About the Author

Joseph G. Correa is a licensed mortgage broker and the founder of Finibi Mortgage, a Florida-based brokerage specializing in home equity, real estate investment financing, and alternative lending strategies for homeowners, business owners, and investors. With more than two decades of experience in mortgage lending, underwriting, and financial structuring, Joseph has helped thousands of borrowers access capital using intelligent, low-risk leverage rather than high-interest consumer debt.

Unlike traditional loan officers who focus only on closing transactions, Joseph's approach is rooted in long-term financial strategy. He believes that mortgages, HELOCs, and credit lines should be used as tools for building wealth, protecting cash flow, and creating financial resilience — not as traps that keep families locked into decades of unnecessary interest payments. This philosophy has made him a trusted advisor for entrepreneurs, real estate investors, and self-employed borrowers who need flexible, modern financing solutions that banks often fail to provide.

Joseph is widely known for his expertise in home equity lines of credit, no-documentation and bank-statement loan programs, investor financing, and creative equity-based strategies such as debt-elimination systems and capital recycling. His ability to translate complex lending rules into simple, actionable guidance has helped homeowners turn idle equity into productive capital for investments, businesses, and passive income.

Through his education platform, Finibi Academy, Joseph has trained tens of thousands of students worldwide in credit, mortgage strategy, real estate financing, and financial independence. His courses and books are used by first-time homeowners, seasoned investors, and financial professionals seeking a clearer, more honest understanding of how modern lending really works.

Joseph created *The Home Equity Wealth Series* to give everyday homeowners the same financial knowledge that banks, hedge funds, and institutional investors use to control capital and minimize risk. His mission is simple: to help people stop guessing, stop fearing debt, and start using smart leverage to build real financial freedom.

When he is not structuring loans or writing, Joseph works with families and investors across the United States to design personalized equity strategies that align with their goals, cash flow, and long-term wealth plans.

The Home Equity Wealth Series Roadmap

The Professional Guide to Using Your Home to Build Financial Freedom

The purpose of *The Home Equity Wealth Series* is to give homeowners the same financial tools and strategies used by banks, investors, and institutions—translated into clear, practical guidance for everyday people. Each book builds on the last, taking you from basic understanding to advanced mastery of how to use home equity safely, intelligently, and profitably across every stage of life.

Book 1 — *HELOC Fundamentals*This book gives you the foundation. You will understand how Home Equity Lines of Credit work, how they are structured, how risk is controlled, and how equity becomes usable capital. The books that follow are designed to help you apply that knowledge to your own situation, your income type, your credit profile, and your long-term financial goals.

Book 2 — *How to Qualify for a HELOC* This book shows you how lenders actually evaluate borrowers. You will learn how credit scores, income, property type, and debt ratios affect approval, limits, and interest rates. You will also learn how to position yourself to qualify for the largest possible credit line at the best possible terms.

Book 3 — *HELOCs for Real Estate Investors* This book focuses on using home equity to buy, rehab, refinance, and scale rental properties. It explains how investors use HELOCs for down payments, renovations, and portfolio growth while keeping cash flow positive and risk controlled.

Book 4 — *Self-Employed HELOC Strategies* Designed for business owners, freelancers, 1099 borrowers, and LLCs, this book explains how bank-statement income, business income, and alternative documentation can be used to qualify for home equity even when traditional tax returns do not reflect true cash flow.

Book 5 — *Credit Mastery for HELOC Approval* This book dives deep into credit strategy. You will learn how utilization, credit mix, and reporting behavior affect HELOC limits and pricing—and how to optimize your credit profile specifically for home equity approval.

Book 6 — *No-Doc & Alternative HELOC Programs* This book covers asset-based HELOCs, no-income-verification options, and non-traditional lending programs for high-net-worth, self-employed, or cash-heavy borrowers who do not fit inside standard underwriting models.

Book 7 — *Using a HELOC to Eliminate Debt* This book teaches how to use home equity to replace high-interest credit cards, personal loans, and auto loans with low-interest revolving credit, allowing borrowers to eliminate debt years faster and save tens of thousands of dollars in interest.

Book 8 — *Using a HELOC to Build Wealth* This book shows how homeowners fund investments, businesses, and passive income streams using HELOCs while maintaining liquidity and controlling risk.

Book 9 — *HELOC Risk Management* This book focuses entirely on safety. You will learn how to structure buffers, cash-flow coverage, rate protection, and leverage limits so your home becomes safer over time—not more vulnerable.

Book 10 — *The Smart Borrower's Home Equity Blueprint* The final book ties everything together into a complete lifetime strategy for using home equity as a personal banking system, investment engine, and financial safety net.

Book 11 — *The Cashflow Accelerator Method*

The Cashflow Accelerator Method is the final transformation stage of *The Home Equity Wealth Series.* While the earlier books teach how to access, qualify for, and safely use home equity, this book teaches how to **weaponize cash flow itself** to permanently eliminate debt and create lasting wealth. Together, these books are designed to turn a single asset—your home—into a lifelong financial advantage. Each volume adds another layer of understanding, allowing you to move from homeowner to capital manager, from borrower to strategist, and from financial stress to long-term stability.

This is not about taking more risk.It is about learning how money really works—and using that knowledge to build financial freedom that lasts.

Educational & Financial Disclaimer

This book is provided for **educational and informational purposes only**. The author and publisher are not engaged in rendering legal, tax, accounting, investment, or financial advice. Although the author is a licensed mortgage broker, the information in this book is intended to provide general education about Home Equity Lines of Credit (HELOCs) and home equity strategy, not personalized financial, legal, or lending advice.

Mortgage programs, underwriting guidelines, interest rates, credit requirements, and home equity products vary by lender, investor, state, and economic conditions, and may change at any time without notice. The examples, calculations, and scenarios presented in this book are hypothetical and are for illustration only. They do not represent guaranteed outcomes or actual loan approvals.

Before making any financial decisions, including applying for a HELOC, refinancing, borrowing against home equity, or using credit for investment or debt repayment, readers should consult with a qualified mortgage professional, financial advisor, tax advisor, or attorney who can evaluate their specific situation.

Risk Disclosure

Borrowing against home equity involves risk. A HELOC is secured by your home, which means failure to make required payments could result in foreclosure or loss of property. This book teaches responsible, conservative, and structured use of home equity, but no financial strategy is risk-free.

Readers are solely responsible for their financial decisions. Neither the author nor the publisher makes any warranties, express or implied, about the accuracy, completeness, or applicability of the information in this book to any individual or situation.

www.ingramcontent.com/pod-product-compliance
Ingram Content Group UK Ltd.
Pitfield, Milton Keynes, MK11 3LW, UK
UKHW020157290926
15471UKWH00005B/922

9 798295 573989